#UsToo
Bridging the Global Gender Gap

Debjani Mukherjee Biswas

Edited by Performance Publishing Group
Cover Design by Performance Publishing Group
Cover photo courtesy of Adobe Stock
Published by Performance Publishing Group May 2018

ISBN: 978-1-946629-27-2 (paperback)

Because of the dynamic nature of the Internet, any web addresses or links contained in this book may have changed since publication and may no longer be valid.

FIRST EDITION

Table of Contents

Introduction

What is #UsToo? It is an initiative, powered by both men and women, launched to bridge the gender gap.

There are four key thoughts driving #UsToo:

1. Our daughters and sisters have as fundamental a right to be safe as our sons and brothers.

2. As we uncover ways in which women (and some men) are abused, our first gut reaction is to blame the group that most of the abusers fall under.

3. Instead, we must tackle the root cause of inequity in gender norms, expectations, and biases.

4. All of us must be part of the solution.

There are two sets of key questions which uncover how, at the core, we feel about this topic.

A. What are your deep-seated beliefs about gender abilities, norms, and 'rules'?

- What have men and women accomplished?

- What are they capable of doing?

- How *should* men and women behave?

B. What are your underlying assumptions about gender power?

- Do you believe that men are more powerful than women?

- Do you believe that women are more powerful than men?

- Do you believe that both men and women are equally powerful?

Ask yourself the power questions about men and women at work, and then, separately, about men and women at home.

Why did you pick up a book which focuses on bridging the gender gap? Is it because you feel that you are at the lower end of the gender spectrum? Or are you going to learn these techniques because you see yourself as a catalyst of change for someone else? Whatever your reason, be very clear as to your *why*. Nietzsche said, 'He who has a why to live for can endure almost any how'.

I am firmly planted on this path because my late father boldly shattered tired gender and cultural stereotypes in order to facilitate my engineering career path. Thanks to his example, I strive to pay it forward with this book, leveraging his strong sense of fairness with logic.

What is your primary reason for bridging the gender gap?

_____

_____

_____

_____

_____

In 2017, the world was shaken to its core by the host of revelations that caused empires in industry after industry to topple. How could this level of sexual harassment and misuse of power have happened? Sometimes for decades? To so many people?

The #MeToo movement, first initiated by the pioneering Tarana Burke, was reintroduced by Hollywood actor Alyssa Milano. Literally thousands of women (and some men) came forward to share their stories. As someone who has herself experienced a #MeToo event as a teenager, I am filled with pride for these courageous people.

I have noticed a subtle shift in the pendulum. Because, so often, men were the abusers, it is becoming more of an 'us versus them' position for many women. In its most simplistic form, the *politically correct* approach for someone like me—a female engineer working on gender equity and inclusion—would be to either vilify or dismiss men. That, however, is not my approach. For me, logic demands that we cannot talk about gender inclusion by excluding about 50% of the population.

I am aware that this is a controversial approach. My mentor taught me to ask, 'What else might be true?' when I find myself arguing for a particular side.

Very simply, this book has one, and only one, purpose.

And that is, to answer the question: How can decent and honorable men and women work together to reduce gender bias and stereotyping, and close the gender gap?

Let me be very clear. I have zero tolerance for the abusers and harassers. They should be caught and punished as justly as possible, both in the eyes of the law and in society. I also have very little respect for the men (and, in some cases, women) who stood by silently for years, fully aware of what was going on behind closed doors.

This book is not for them.

This is for you, average Joe and regular Jenna, who want to do the right thing so that our inequitable society with its global epidemic of broken systems starts healing. What is a broken system? It is a structural or societal set up where manipulation of power is allowed or even approved. For example, a luxury hotel where a guest feels that he has the 'right' to sexually harass a maid coming in to clean his room. And she realizes that her job is at risk if she complains about this injustice.

How does the healing begin? The healing begins by answering some deep and basic questions.

1.   What has been your experience of gender?

2.   How gender biased are you?

3. Where did your biases come from?

4. Which biases will you reduce first as an individual?

5. What actions will you take one level up[i]?

    a. First, by recognizing broken systems

    b. Next, by uncovering dysfunctional pathways to success

    c. Finally, by committing to changing them, one step at a time

6. What bridges will you build to replace these broken pathways?

7. With whom will you share the messages of this new learning and path?

Boldly Shattering Tired Gender Stereotypes

When I was born, the youngest of four girls, someone came to my father and said, 'We are so sorry that you had yet another girl'. My father replied, 'Call me in 20 years and tell me how your son's doing. And I will tell you how my daughter's doing'.[ii]

How lucky was I to have such an advocate from the moment I was born? He is one of the main reasons I am writing this book: to honor the kind and decent fathers, husbands, sons, brothers, friends, and family who work, sometimes quietly, to boldly shatter tired gender stereotypes.

FIGURE 1. Author as a teenager with her father Debu Mukherjee

This photo was taken with my father fourteen years later. Don't know if he ever called that friend! As my good friend Jo[iii] commented:

'I see a lot more in this picture than first meets the eye. To start, the quiet pride of a father who has gently nurtured his daughter on a nontraditional path, seeing the results of all his years of effort in a society that does not encourage girls to strike out, leave alone aim for any sort of career. It required, back then, a solid commitment from the father to 'not compartmentalize', 'not discriminate', to encourage based on ability. It took a lot of guts to take the path he did. A generation back, there were not many fathers who had the broad vision and foresight to do what he did. Mothers, perhaps. Fathers, not many. He brought you a very long way, Debjani'.

My Journey

But you don't look like an engineer!

When I was fifteen, I graduated high school from an all-girls convent school. At the age of sixteen, I looked up to see thirty-nine boys – and me – in engineering school at the fiercely competitive Indian Institute of Technology[iv]. I truly experienced firsthand the gender differences—what it felt like to be one of the only females in an exclusively male normed world. For five years, this was my reality. Naturally, my choice of career also led me to similar work environments for over twenty years. I experienced both the negative and positive (yes, sometimes strongly positive) effects of gender stereotyping over and over again.

What else?

After living in Asia until my twenties, I moved to the U.S. Once again, I experienced being *different* due to the way I spoke, the color of my skin, and cultural norms or beliefs. I asked myself, 'Does being different work for or against one?' A simple question with a complex, multilayered answer.

After over twenty years in corporate roles, I was laid off from my job as an executive in a Fortune 50 company. Though it was quite a shock at the time, it turned out to be, unexpectedly, a huge gift. Our son asked a simple question. 'You have wanted to write a book for the longest time. What are you waiting for?' Though I had never written anything more than corporate expense statements, I decided to go for it.

The journey to this moment in time.

In 2013, my first book *Unleash the Power of Diversity* was published. An engineering friend had Googled it and informed me that as a first time, self-published, 'no name' author, I would sell 250 or fewer copies of my book. Bought, he added, by my family and friends for the most part.

So I wrote a book entirely for myself—almost like a diary—about the way I had experienced bias and stereotyping and how we could be more culturally competent as individuals and organizations. I firmly believed that my friend's observation would, indeed, be the fate of my book; yet the world had other things in store for me. A colleague persuaded me to try to get my book into stores. Lo and behold, Barnes & Noble accepted my simple two-page application and selected *Unleash the Power of Diversity* for bookstores all over the U.S. Later that year, I started a U.S. Barnes & Noble book tour.

Somewhere along the way, I developed a vision for a series of books on inclusion of culture, style, gender, and generation.

Emboldened yet completely mystified by this first sign of success, I was shocked when *Miserably Successful No More* (the second book in the series) became an international bestseller in 2017 and hit #1 on Amazon in its category in the first few days.

My career morphed into presenting keynotes on inclusion to large groups of people at conferences and corporate events all over the world. Oh and by the way, remember that '250 book limit' comment from my engineering friend? A few years ago, during an International Women's Day keynote, we sold my 'lifelong limit' in books in just one day!

What is the gender norm for humility versus self-belief?

Why do I share this story, which as I read it sounds so boastful that I cringe and want to immediately delete it? It highlights how an otherwise self-confident and previously successful woman can believe the limits that other people set for her. Incidentally, there are many successful men who suffer from this distorted mirror view of themselves also, believing naysayers around them.

By and large, as women, we tend to downplay instead of owning our success. That is the first tired gender stereotype that I want to shatter.

As my good friend Linda coached me two years into this surreal ride, it was time to learn to accept, not discount, positive outcomes. I kept saying, 'How lucky I am that X happened, and Y happened'. And Linda taught me to acknowledge the hard work, grit, and perseverance that had got me to this point, using a simple technique. She said, 'For every success that you have achieved, put my name instead of yours. Say "Linda wrote a book, and X and Y happened." Now, tell me. Is Linda "lucky"?'

Suddenly, I realized what she was trying to tell me. When others succeeded, I could see so clearly how much effort they had put into it, yet I was unable to see it in myself. Reader, remember this learning when you take your self-assessment later in this book.

Finally, I share this in case you, the reader, are going through a particularly rough patch in your career or life. I had to go through both professional and personal (health related) traumas in order to get here. And *here* is so much better than the life I would have lived if I hadn't been laid off. Life can be strange sometimes. The tipping point that made this transition possible was a robust three-legged stool of a support system.[v]

And so here we are. This time, I am again going to write the book that I really want to while expressing my views and hopefully furthering my life mission: Learning, helping, teaching — with graceful flawed authenticity.

Please read it with eyes wide open. I hope you will disagree with me because that will mean you are using your mind and thinking independently. We can both share diverse opinions and come to a bridging point in the middle.

Reflection Questions from This Topic

- Who has boldly shattered tired gender stereotypes for you?

- For whom (if anyone) have you boldly shattered tired gender stereotypes?

- What is one action you can take to reduce biases using #UsToo at work or at home?

Define the Gender Gap

In order to heal and bridge the gender gap, we need to understand what the gender gap is and how our own views and experiences form this gap.

What is the gender gap?

Before we look at the gender gap, let's list some of your views and experiences:

Gender is _____

_____

I encourage you to go beyond the obvious anatomical definitions of male and female, and think characteristics and behaviors.

Some words associated with 'like a girl' are:

_____

_____

Some words associated with 'like a boy' are:

_____

_____

Some words associated with 'like a man' are:

_____

_____

Some words associated with 'like a woman' are:

_____

_____

How have you experienced the gender gap?

How old were you when you first realized that gender mattered? What was the context in which it happened?

_____

_____

_____

_____

_____

What is the gender gap? Describe all areas in which you see a gap.

_____

_____

_____

_____

How have you personally experienced the gender gap at work or at home?

_____

_____

_____

Personal ask: We are in the data-gathering phase for *Gender: The Ultimate Power Paradox* (2019), my full-length book on gender diversity. Please fill out the form at **Contact@Coachieve.Us** Your responses will be anonymous, of course, and will help us in our research.

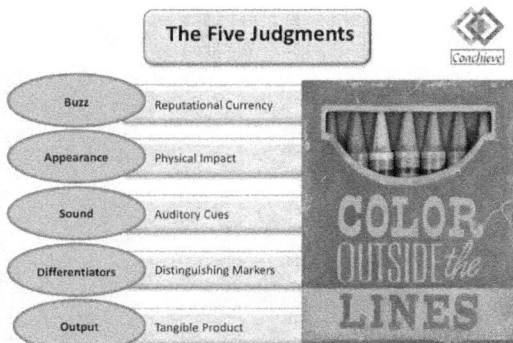

The Five Judgments

Buzz	Reputational Currency
Appearance	Physical Impact
Sound	Auditory Cues
Differentiators	Distinguishing Markers
Output	Tangible Product

Source: Unleash the Power of Diversity" 2013 Biswas http://amzn.to/160FcZa

Notice the Gender Gap

Before we can begin to reduce the gender gap, we must notice how we contribute to it. Awareness is always the first step.

What are my gender values, norms, and beliefs?

The tool we will use is The Five Judgments (an original bias and stereotyping framework I introduced in *Unleash the Power of Diversity*, 2013)[vi]. I ask you to apply it specifically to gender bias. The principles apply for race, generation, style, and other aspects, but let's focus on gender for now. Do not assume that you will be biased against the opposite gender alone.

When I wrote my first book, my editors told me that every time I spoke about someone in power, I used the pronoun *he*. This was a sign of my unconscious bias that people in power would be men. Take the self-assessment, and be open to what it shows you.

The Five Judgments©

There are five judgments that we make about people, several of which have nothing to do with the caliber of their work or their output. They are:

Reputational Currency: Long before you personally interact with a person, you have preconceived notions about the group to which they belong. This could be based on your values, parental and peer group influences, word of mouth, or social media. If there is no data about this person, you will make the first judgment based on stereotyping and unconscious biases. What is your belief about gender? How would you fill out the sentence 'like a girl/boy is _____ and like a woman/man is _____ to me'? If a female executive is strong, is she aggressive? If a male nurse attends to you, is his choice of career feminine? Only you will answer this. Be brutally honest.

Physical Impact: As soon as you interact with this person, you form a second judgment based on two key components of physical impact — her visual appeal and freshness quotient. Visual appeal relates to her innate physical attributes, as well as attire and accessories. *Should* a woman be slim? Does a man with white hair look *distinguished* ... or old? Apparent age range, perceived attractiveness, trendiness, power, physical stance, and presence are all part of this judgment. What role should physical impact have on a person's success?

By the way, as you are analyzing how you judge men and women based on these judgments, assess yourself also. What are the tired stereotypes in *your mind* about how you should look and dress? Apply this to all the judgments.

Auditory Cues: The third judgment is formed based on pitch and tone of voice, giggles versus laughter, as well as the volume, speed, and number of words used. Unconsciously held beliefs cause us to judge the same thing differently depending on our frame of reference. There is a gender context to auditory cues: women tend to apologize more than men, thus reducing their perceived power. How do you judge others based on how they sound? How do you think you sound in terms of power? Are you concise or long winded? People will judge you based on whether you interrupt or apologize, or even how high pitched your voice is. Superficial? Yes. Happening? Also, yes.

Distinguishing Markers: What is unique or different about the opposite gender? Your gender? This fourth judgment is particularly critical in gender exploration. A distinguishing marker in one situation may not be categorized as such in another. Distinguishing markers can be behavioral, situational, or physical. What is your distinguishing marker? Are you a person of great talent who has obsessed about some small physical imperfection for decades?

Media has a powerful impact on gender bias by making us assign different distinguishing markers to men and women. If a lead actress's distinguishing marker is almost always her beauty and youth and a lead actor's distinguishing marker is how well he acts, there is clearly something wrong with the system and society that put these unspoken rules in place.

Judge yourself by your own standard, not society's gender stereotype of who or what you are or should be.

Work Product: The fifth judgment relates to our output – its quality and how original it is, as well as how much we can produce in a given amount of time. The most interesting learning here is that, typically, four judgments occur before one even starts to examine a person's output.

These judgments result in an overall 'score' and placement of that individual, which can have a powerful effect on their success or failure. This critical first impression is supplemented over time by perceived future behavior and performance. First impressions are often more important than actual results.

Reflection Questions from This Topic

- Using the gender lens, which of the five judgments was most eye opening for you?
- In which judgment did you find yourself more gender neutral or equitable?
- What are your tired gender stereotypes?

Where did our gender values, norms, and biases come from?

This is not a complete listing, but based on personal observations, research, and informal data gathering, here are some sources of gender norms and biases:

- Media messaging around gender identity and power

- Social Media – a twenty-first century phenomenon

- Advertising – commercial sales of products and concepts

- Entertainment – movies, television, theater, and magazines

- News – all electronic and printed news sources

- Religion

- Family and friends

- Political leadership

- Societal norms in general

- Career messaging

- Static or one-way delivery of words, images, and sounds

  - Books and literature (prose and poetry)

  - Art and visual images

  - Music – subtle messaging in songs

- Intersection of gender with other diversity sources

  - Culture

  - Style

  - Generation

As this is a condensed book, I will not go into each of these areas in depth. However, for the sake of reflection, this is a fairly comprehensive list.

Here are some of the key sources:

Media
In a world of electronic shackles, we are bound to media at multiple levels. You can see how I have separated social media from news and entertainment. However, there is clearly an overlap between some of these sources.

Don't underestimate the huge impact of the movies we watch, the TV shows we allow our children to see, or the music we listen to. Do you know that thousands of women wept during *Wonder Woman* because, for the very first time, they were seeing a female super hero as a metaphor for their own power? How has *Black Panther* changed the diorama not just from the cultural lens but also from the gender lens? Typically, what is the gender for the 'tech' support for a superhero? Who was originally the 'Q' to James Bond? Fast forward to the *Black Panther*. The 'tech gizmo genius' is a young African woman, the princess, in fact, of the fictitious 'Wakanda', worlds apart from other 'princesses' we have seen in movies for decades.

Google the words of Cindy Lauper's 'Girls Just Want to Have Fun' (one of my all-time favorites, by the way) and compare them to Idina Menzel's 'Let It Go' from the movie *Frozen*. Eye opening? When the songwriting team of 'Let it Go', Robert and Kristen Anderson Lopez, were accepting the Oscar for the song, they dedicated it to their little girls, on whose behalf they had written these lyrics.

While the visual aspect of art impacts our eyes a certain way, obviously when we watch a movie or play a video game, we are getting visual cues as well. These inputs may depend on how scantily dressed the female avatar is, or how 'macho' the hero of the movie is perceived to be.

Family and friends
Research suggests that a person's primary adult caregiver — until recently one's mother, more often than not, in traditional households — has a huge impact on one's values, norms, and beliefs. I was graced with ignorance about how men and women were 'supposed' to behave because my mother is very strong and practical, and my gentle father would hover over our cribs at night, just to check that we were breathing nicely.

Media Stereotyping Example

I was attending a Jan Chozen Bays[vii] workshop in the Zen Buddhist monastery a few years ago. Dr. Bays showed us eye-opening images of women from different countries in advertisements, movies, and Old Masters paintings. She pointed out the irony of a country where girls become bulimic or anorexic in an attempt to look like size 0 models; and the national average is size 14. These behaviors are both dangerous and ineffective. As a society, we spend billions of dollars on diet products; yet the obesity crisis is at an all-time high. Further, this is a root cause for related mental health issues as well.

As parents, we are often unaware of how strongly our behaviors (more than our words) impact gender bias. I have always loved mathematics, and my mother has always been the numbers person in our household. My father, though forced into a STEM[viii] education because of reverse gender stereotyping, was a historian and musician at heart. These nonverbal messages had, and continue to have, a profound impact on how I experience gender in the world.

Intersection of multiple sources of gender bias: Let's say you were born in a country where there is a tradition of females having limited or no careers. Obviously, being a homemaker is an important and valuable role for a spouse or partner. Now let's say you add the other aspect of low socioeconomic status (SES). Will that force the female to seek outside work, and thus change the gender norm for that household? What about age? Will a baby boomer couple from that culture have the same gender norms as their millennial offspring? Unlikely.

Reader, I know you feel like we have only scratched the surface of this topic. I agree completely. Yet the purpose of a condensed book is to start you on your journey. So please look at the list of sources, and select the ones that have impacted your gender biases the most. You can look at both the Five Judgments reflections and the list in this chapter before you answer these reflection questions.

Reflection Questions from This Topic

- Who or what has been the most powerful sources of gender stereotypes for you?

- How will you inoculate yourself from their/its messaging in the future?

- How will you use #UsToo to reject outdated gender stereotypes and encourage both men *and* women to be strong *and* empathetic?

Bridge the Gender Gap

We learned about the Five Judgments and how gender biased we are. You reflected on at least one area where you still make some kind of inequitable rule in your mind, based solely on a person's gender. Finally, we must look at real steps to heal and bridge the gender gap. First, we start with stereotypes.

How can I reduce biases and boldly shatter tired stereotypes?

I was speaking at an international conference in London a few years ago about how successful women often define themselves by their weight. I asked the audience to pledge with me that we will no longer let our body images be dictated by unrealistic images of skinny models. The audience loved it and clapped enthusiastically. While watching a video of this event, a close friend applauded my statement. Literally a few minutes later, she said, 'Can I give you some advice? If you were twenty pounds lighter, people would listen to you more'.

That, dear reader, is an example of mixed gender messaging and deep-rooted gender bias.

Now let us examine a practical global toolkit for bridging the gender gap at an individual level. It is called the Diversity Foray and was introduced in *Unleash the Power of Diversity*[ix] in 2013.

The Diversity Foray©

Let's recap where we are in our gender journey. First, we asked ourselves why we wanted to close the gender gap. It could be for a child, a sibling, a friend, or a colleague. Next, we examined our deep-rooted beliefs and (often unconscious) gender biases using a framework called the Five Judgments. We then looked at some of the most powerful sources of gender bias: our parents, media, and cultural background to name a few.

We have now come to the most powerful question of all: So what?

I repeat: So what?

Is this going to be one of those books that you pick up, read, say a couple nice things about (maybe even write a five-star Amazon review), and then walk away?

No. That is not an option. If no finite, tangible, action occurs to bridge the gender gap, then you and I have wasted our time together. And that would just be foolish.

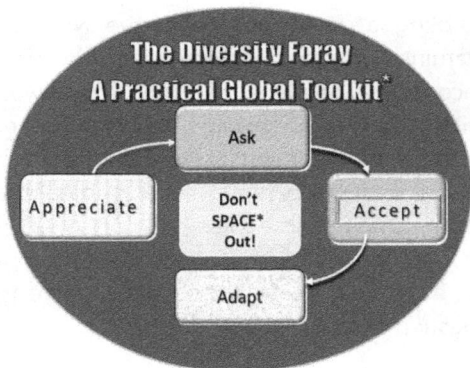

The Diversity Foray
A Practical Global Toolkit*

Ask

Appreciate

Don't
SPACE*
Out!

Accept

Adapt

The Diversity Foray© –
A Practical Toolkit of Dos and Don'ts

When I was designing this toolkit, I suddenly realized that all the dos started with an 'A'. And there were four of them: * Ask * Accept * Adapt and * Appreciate. So I called these four A's a 'foray', which serendipitously means an exploration or journey. Everything fitted in nicely.

That being said, in the gender context, I am taking some poetic (prose?) license with the third 'A', i.e., adapt. If you are a Hammer[x] (a blunt, highly assertive person), by all means try to adapt. However, if you are a Brush (a soft person, sometimes a people pleaser, often a conflict avoider), please adapt to how *adaptive* you are! In other words, 'assert' instead of agreeing. Let others 'adapt' to you for a change, instead of the other way around.

DOs

To summarize, the four dos are:

Ask

Powerful questions are the first step to bridging the gender gap. We have already asked some guided questions in this book around your personal norms and biases. Now ask questions at a societal and structural level. Let the questions become uncomfortable.

One powerful question would be: Why is it that some powerful men were able to abuse their power for decades without other men (and, in some cases, women) *who knew*, stepping

49

forward? What systems can I put in place in my organization to make it safe for people to speak up? What is the gender gap in pay? How did the U.K. uncover the huge gender inequity between top male and female newscasters in 2017? What are the keys to reducing inequities? If transparency is one of the keys, how transparent am I in my professional and personal life?

Accept

There are some gender battles I choose not to fight. When initiating change, accept that there are some people who are sexist and will work hard to maintain gender inequity because they are on the 'right' end of it. In the same way that a really rich person doesn't buy a book about how to retire comfortably in a few years, so also these people feel that there is nothing to be gained by gender equity.

Make a logical cost benefit analysis. Is the reason for their inertia sheer ignorance, denial, or a self-serving bias? Is it worth the effort involved in trying to change their attitude? If the answer is no, move on. Accept that some efforts are wasted on the truly misguided or self-centered.

Adapt
Where do you fall in the gender spectrum? Let's say you are a male Gen Xer with a female millennial boss. Are you labeling or categorizing her a certain way for being assertive? If she was a male boss, would you use the same labels? Recognize your implicit biases and try to adapt your behaviors until these new approaches take shape. Be aware that you will take some time to go up the Ladder of Competence[xi], from unconscious incompetence to conscious incompetence all the way up to unconscious competence.

Appreciate
True gender appreciation lies in the synergy that results from diverse perspectives. I am reminded of the car manufacturer whose female engineer designed a very inexpensive

part that allowed a woman to hang her purse and groceries in the car and resulted in a huge uptick in sales. And their leaders were consistent and vocal in their appreciation of this innovative engineer who could see beyond the horsepower and V8 engine to what a large percentage of the population needed. Appreciate someone's gender characteristics carefully if they are true and add to the diversity of thinking in your group or team.

DON'Ts

There are five don'ts. Since I like acronyms and they are easy to remember, the five don'ts are a reminder not to S.P.A.C.E. out. In other words, don't * Shun * Patronize * Assume * Crumble or * Escalate. Let's look at how each of the don'ts comes into play. Please note that this is the biggest barrier to bridging the gender gap. *If there is one page to bookmark, it is this one.*

Shun

I was watching an old movie the other day involving people at an exclusive country club.

It was clear that women were not allowed. Sadly, decades later, we are subtler in our approach, but there are still areas where we don't think that one gender quite fits. I call this the 'second best syndrome' – where role rigidity means that we assign 'best' status to one gender and the other is *always a poor second*. This phenomenon has a powerful impact on gender dynamics; as analyzed in 'Gender: the Ultimate Power Paradox'[xii].

'Shun' Example: The 'Second Best Syndrome' of Role Rigidity

A mother and her two-year-old son were flying home one day when the flight attendant came over. The pilot had agreed to meet with the child, in order to present him with the airline's Little Wings badge or pin. The little boy was, of course, very excited. When the boy met the pilot, his eyes widened because the pilot was a female.

The boy cried all the way home as they drove back from the airport. Why? Because the pilot wasn't a 'real' pilot? Why? Because 'real pilots are men'.

What kind of society do we live in that a *two-year-old* boy has such a strong conviction as to which gender a pilot should be?

When sharing this story with us, the boy's mother was visibly concerned. She believes strongly, and vocally, in gender equity. How could her son have developed this bias?[xiii]

Patronize

Have you noticed an increasing trend to show men as impractical, foolish, and clumsy in U.S. advertising, particularly in television commercials? For example, men at a party are recklessly swinging from heights near a swimming pool and playing foolish games while their savvy wives are ready to call for medical insurance. There are multiple examples of this. Here's the interesting observation. If even half of these commercials did such blatant gender stereotyping for females, there would be an absolute furor. So, why is it okay to patronize any one gender and repeatedly portray them this way?

Assume

Do you assume that every member will show all the typical characteristics of that gender group? As you climb up the slippery slope of generalization, be very careful not to end up annoying the person or group you are trying to compliment. This has happened to me several times. Yes, I am a female. No, I am not soft and kind—except as a mother, and even in that role, not always! I am also highly competitive by nature. So for you, my male colleague, to compliment me on how 'adaptive and collaborative I am, being a woman' is not a positive for me *in any way*.

Crumble

There is a famous French comedian who relentlessly makes fun of a group of mothers that live close to her comedy club. She parodies how these women spoil their grown sons into a sense of entitlement. Even worse, they also expect their daughters-in-law to wait on their sons hand and foot. Thus, creating a vicious cycle of overwork and lack of consideration. When approached by the media to stop targeting these mothers, the artist retorted, 'As soon as they stop behaving that way, I will stop making jokes about them!'

There is a difference between adapting and crumbling. One moves the agenda forward; the other is capitulation out of fear.

Escalate

This is the single most important reason for me to write this book. I believe that we must escalate to the fullest level possible when something immoral, offensive, abusive, or unethical (obviously, illegal falls in this group as well) occurs. At the same time, I am asking us to recognize the huge emotional residue that we may carry inside us, naturally, following recent revelations. Do we get so touchy, sometimes, that we misinterpret the slightest, most innocent, gesture, word, or tone as being gender inequitable?

#UsToo was designed so we can recognize warning signs of escalation, cemented into us versus them positions. I would suggest speaking to the people that are beginning to escalate in a straightforward and caring manner. Are you getting a strong visceral reaction? Good. First, please see the comments by people all over the world about their perception of this phenomenon.

Next, ask yourself these two questions:

- Can I listen as if I might be wrong?

- What else might be true?

Reflection Questions from This Topic

- Which of the dos will you practice putting into action – * Ask * Accept * Adapt/Assert (depending on your communication style) or * Appreciate?

- Which don't is easy for you to see – * Shun * Patronize * Assume * Crumble or * Escalate? Which of these don'ts made you feel a little uncomfortable?

#UsToo© Conclusion and Action Planning

If we agree that both our daughters and sons – and we ourselves – are entitled to equally safe and successful futures, we are committing to #UsToo.

This is my expectation of you from this moment onwards: that you will be aware of, and change, subtle inequities in the way you speak and think about, or act on, important gender topics. Use a lens of healing the wrongs that have been uncovered in #MeToo and the work of the Silence Breakers, and then spread the movement to help bridge gender gaps in your personal and professional life.

Further, I expect you to be selective in how you accept the biased messaging of your internal and external world. Throughout the book, you have looked at your own tired stereotypes. I hope that after reading this book you will change at least one outdated behavior and belief.

I ask you to apply #UsToo to both your professional and personal life. Make sure your sons know their way around a kitchen. Model the fact that being strong and empathetic means it is okay to be vulnerable. Teach them the value of continuing to have * Grit[xiv] and * Gravitas, and leaning into the discomfort (for some of them) of showing * Grace with it.

As parents, instructors, colleagues, and mentors, teach your daughters that we expect them to have * Grit * Gravitas and * Grace also. They do not need to give up power in order to be liked. Instead of continuously emphasizing their softness, appearance, and obedience, society should applaud their courage, abilities, and resilience. More women should learn the art and science of saying 'no' and speaking the uncomfortable truth.

Let us move together into a world where this book is no longer needed. That would be my biggest sense of achievement.

When Justin Trudeau, the Prime Minister of Canada, formed his Cabinet a few years ago, he was asked why his Cabinet was equally peopled by men and women. He answered simply, 'Because it's 2015'. That was how many years ago? How are we doing, in all walks of life, on this metric?

It is no longer a question of whether we can afford to heal and bridge this gap with #UsToo. It is a question of whether we can afford not to.

We have reached that point in our journey where our ways must part. Thank you for your openness, your attention, and your commitment to actions[xv].

I see you. You are as me, caught in what Covey[xvi] called the 'thick of thin things'. Take a deep breath, as I did a moment ago. *There is no moment in time but this one*, fleeting and ephemeral; powerful in its fragility.

Together, shall we seize *this moment*, and make it *momentous*?

All movements start with a single small step.

What will yours be?[xvii]

**Individual #UsToo Commitment
to Concrete, Tangible Actions**

I applaud you for having read this book with an open mind. Now it's time to commit to at least one specific and meaningful action to bridge the gender gap.

I often divide change actions into *doing* and *being* commitments.

For example:

- I will continue to write books and articles on gender inclusion, bringing as much of my background of head (engineering) and heart (personal style and emotional intelligence training) into the equation. That's a ***doing*** commitment.

- I will also be more aware of my visceral reactions to opposing viewpoints, forcing myself to listen without reacting or responding. To just listen. This is a ***being*** commitment. I promise to *be* more open to differing viewpoints (as long as they do not violate any moral or ethical norms).

What are some individual actions you commit to taking to bridge the gender gap?

They could be as simple as sharing the learning from this book with others (doing) or being aware of your own language (being). You may then move from being (awareness of your language) to doing (changing that language).

A senior executive trains her son and daughter to be more gender neutral when discussing occupations. Instead of saying 'fireman', she uses the term 'firefighter'. Instead of 'policeman', she says 'police officer'.

If may seem like a small shift, but language is powerful.

DOING

1. In social media interactions, I will use the #UsToo phrase and explain it to others whenever I experience an *us versus them* tone to gender comments and interactions. Specifically, I will help heal the gender gap by:

_____

_____

_____

_____

2. I commit to bridging the system-wide gender gap in pay, opportunities, biases, and stereotypes by: _____

_____

_____

_____

BEING

I commit to:_____

_____

_____

_____

#UsToo 'One Level Up' Action Planning

Please don't think about this until you have worked on your individual commitments. Change occurs one small bite-sized piece at a time. When you have consistently changed the *being* commitment into an unconscious habit and are *doing* what you can to bridge the gender gap, please revisit this page.

My #UsToo 'One Level Up' action is to add this lens to inclusion and diversity consulting and coaching. When I walk into an organization, I will do a scavenger hunt for artifacts of organizational equity. I will research how many females are on their board of directors. I will examine their 'high-potential' development processes and understand the basis on which career decisions are made.

As a reminder, we defined 'One Level Up' in the first chapter. It is the action which takes your individual effort and raises it to the collective, more powerful level.

My 'One Level Up' action is:

_____

_____

_____

_____

About the Author

Internationally bestselling author and Power Leader Debjani Biswas has a unique combination of executive and corporate experience (20+ years at PepsiCo, TAS, TI) and education (B.S. Chemical Engineering, MBA, MS Org. Strategy). She received the 2017 GDAACC Award in Journalism for 'Diversity Beyond Boundaries' and is a 2013 NAPW Woman of the Year. She is currently CEO and Founder of Coachieve, LLC, which specializes in inclusion and leadership solutions. Biswas also serves on the Board of Directors of her engineering alumni organization IIT-NT.

Change Agent: Six years ago, an executive in a Fortune 50 company, Ms. Biswas realized she was part of a global epidemic of the 'miserably successful'. Biswas then embarked on a journey of self-discovery, transforming herself into an internationally bestselling author, keynote speaker, and trusted strategist for CEOs and leaders. Her first book was selected by Barnes & Noble stores. She later completed a U.S. Barnes & Noble book tour. Her second book, *Miserably Successful No More,* was ranked #1 on Amazon in the U.S. for its category and is an international bestseller. Her groundbreaking and original frameworks are being utilized in over twenty countries.

Unleash the Power of Diversity and *Miserably Successful No More* have both been endorsed by Marshall Goldsmith, the Thinkers50 Award Winner for Most Influential Leader Thinker in the World, and the bestselling author of *What Got You Here Won't Get You There*.

Key Platform: What is the business impact of inclusion and respect in the workplace? Emotional intelligence, particularly self-awareness and interpersonal skills, are integral to our personal and professional evolution. A certified emotional intelligence practitioner, Biswas also applies an engineering mindset of data harvesting and pattern recognition to complex business situations.

International Keynotes, Events, and Media Presence includes:

- National Summit for Educational Equity 2017 – Conference Opening Keynote

- Union Pacific 'Aero' Conference Keynote – The Power of Engagement and Inclusion

- Texas Instruments '#Workplaces that Work for Women Work for All' – IWD 2018

- Ericsson U.S. HQ Keynote – 'Diversity in the Networked Society'

- Takeda Pharmaceuticals U.S. HQ Keynote – 'Harnessing the Power of Diversity'

- IEEE Women in Engineering International Leadership Conference

- INWIC Celebration of Women in Computing & Tech Conference Keynote

- University of New Hampshire STEM Center Launch Keynote, Manchester

- Kennecott Rio Tinto Keynote – 'Leveraging Diversity for Business Results'

- International Coach Federation Global Conference Speaker, London, U.K.

- National Alliance for Partnerships in Equity (NAPE)* Diversity Consultant

- Episcopal School of Dallas – Annual Diversity Celebration Keynote

- Decade for Change 'Domestic Violence' Conference TV/Radio Media Facilitator

- Society for Human Resource Management NT Conference Speaker, Denton USA

Media:
- Dallas Morning News: Business Headline Trending Book Review

- IIM Americas Newsletter: 'Meet a Thought Leader, Debjani Biswas'

- Business Press Review: 'Book Challenges People To Look Inside Themselves'

- Sharp Heels Magazine Interview: 'The Impact of Self Awareness on Success'

- Radio: Multiple Programs and Interviews including ESPN, CBS, KRLD, and iHeart Radio

Testimonials from around the world include:

- Austria – 'A brilliant and very inspirational woman'.

- Australia – 'Learning from her ideas influences my thinking in powerful ways'.

- Finland – 'An inspirational role model who contributes to making the world a better place'.

- Germany – 'A female engineer, tremendously authentic impressions, ideas, advice'.

- India – 'An amazingly easy read, Debjani has couched years of learning in a remarkably simple style'.

- Thailand – 'You'll find yourself examining options to improve everyday interactions'.

- Japan – 'I believe Debjani Biswas is living and walking diversity'.

- Malaysia – 'A unique engineering principles approach to cross cultural effectiveness'.

- Nigeria – 'The first word that comes to mind is "brilliant". An inspiration'.

- United Kingdom – 'Mind shifting insights and a professional and personal toolkit'.

- United States – 'A woman of amazing intelligence, managerial courage, and strategic vision'.

Sample keynote videos available at www.coachieve.us

For more information on Coachieve (**www.coachieve.us**) keynotes, diversity and leadership solutions (assessments, executive coaching, workshops, and consulting), contact our team at **contact@coachieve.us**.

Unleash the Power of Diversity and *Miserably Successful No More* are available on Amazon. 'Gender: The Ultimate Power Paradox', 2019 TBD.

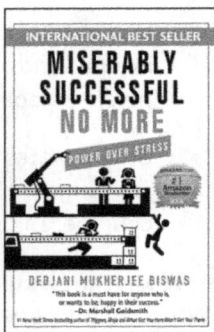

Acknowledgements

This book is dedicated to my father 'Bappi', the late Deba Priya Mukherjee. Wish you were here to share this surreal journey. The way you boldly shattered the 'second best syndrome' for your daughters powers my support of #UsToo.

Thank you to all those who believed in me when there was no logical reason to do so.

A leader I know once said, 'There are three types of people. Those who try to make you feel small or diminish you by acts of omission or commission. Then there are those who support you as you are today. Finally, there are those who can see the you that you may one day aspire to become'. She added, 'If you find the third kind of person, keep them very close to you'.

How lucky I am in the richness of so many who, from the beginning, have seen 'the person that I may one day aspire to become'.

For family who are the best of friends, for friends who have become family.

With each book I feel, more deeply, the loss of precious ones who left us behind. Dadumoni, Baba, Ma, Bangur Mama, Kudy Rani, Jodee.

For colleagues from multiple worlds: IIT, IIM, TAS, TI, ICF, and UTD.

A special note of appreciation to my volunteer editors Barry Pruitt, Ellen Linden, Niket Biswas, Sandra Hoffman and Sheila Franzen. You read this book at so many levels: strategic and technical, from the head and the heart; for accuracy and impact. Thank you is inadequate, really.

Michelle Prince and the wonderful Performance Publishing Group editors and cover designers: I so appreciate your patience, skills and can-do approach to making this book a reality.

To everyone who says 'I want to write a book one day', please believe me: if I can, so can you. We need to hear your opinions and learn from your words.

And finally, for every one of you who has shattered tired gender stereotypes, thank you! Future generations will move forward smoothly because of your acts of courage.

References

i.   'One level up' refers to taking a solution to a higher domain. For example, if in an organization, a marketing person tries to improve the work for marketing alone, that is at her level. If on the other hand, she does things to make the entire company succeed, she is taking it 'one level up'. The same is true of individual change. We can first improve our awareness and reduce our biases. Then, taking it 'one level up', we can positively impact our colleagues, our children, friends – to the point of actually shifting entire cultures, if enough of us persist in this path.

ii.   In order to be accurate, I have repeated my late father's comment verbatim. Of course as related by my mother, as I was only a baby then! His statement might be misconstrued as adversarial. As if he was saying to his friend, 'My daughter will be better than your son.' I, however, never saw him putting other people down – this example was to show his total and unconditional support of his daughter's well-being.

iii. 'Jo' refers to my friend Shirish Joshi. Thank you so much for your thoughtful analysis of this picture, and of my late father's impact on my life and career.

iv. Rebecca Leung, 'Imported from India', CBS News, https://www.cbsnews.com/news/imported-from-india/.

v. Debjani Mukherjee Biswas, *Miserably Successful No More: Power over Stress*, Performance Publishing, 2017, http://amzn.to/2puP3sH.

vi. Debjani Mukherjee Biswas, *Unleash the Power of Diversity: Multi Cultural Competence for Business Results*, Author House, 2013, http://amzn.to/160FcZz.

vii. Jan Chozen Bays, *Mindful Eating: A Guide to Rediscovering a Healthy and Joyful Relationship with Food*, Shambala Publishing, 2009.

References

viii. Science Technology Engineering and Mathematics.

ix. Biswas, *Unleash the Power of Diversity*. See previous link. Also in select Barnes & Noble stores.

x. Biswas, *Miserably Successful No More*, 'Are you a Hammer or a Brush?' See previous link.

xi. "Four Stages of Competence", Wikipedia, https://en.wikipedia.org/wiki/Four_stages_of_competence.

xii. Debjani Mukherjee Biswas, *Gender the Ultimate Power Paradox*, Performance Publishing. 2019 TBD.

xiii. This is a true story. I personally heard it a few months ago.

xiv. Greatness comes from * Grit * Gravitas and * Grace. Biswas, *Gender the Ultimate Power Paradox*, Performance Publishing. 2019 TBD.

xv. Please fill out the action statements at the end of the book and ask someone close to you to hold you to them.

xvi. The late Stephen M. R. Covey, author of *The Seven Habits of Highly Effective People* and multiple bestselling books.

xvii. Loyal and observant readers will recognize the ending as similar to my previous books. This is intentional.